CW00498980

The Ultin Inspector Calls' GCSE Revision Guide & Quote Book

100+ Inspector Calls Quotes with Language Analysis, Context, and Practice Questions for English Literature GCSE 9-1

Jonty Purvis

CONTENTS

ACKNOWLEDGMENTS

Thanks to our friends Greg, Peter, and Thomas – Your help as always has been invaluable.

Moreover, a big thanks to all the students we've spoken to over the years. Without you we wouldn't know where to start when it comes to writing revision guides.

1) INTRODUCTION

Welcome to our comprehensive GCSE English Literature study guide to "An Inspector Calls" by J.B. Priestley. This guide is designed to help you delve into the world of early 20th-century England, providing an extensive examination of over 100 key quotes, literary techniques, and historical context that will equip you to excel in your studies and examinations. Whether you are revising for your final GCSE exam, or have only just started reading the play, this study guide will be an indispensable companion as you explore the complex themes, timeless messages, and striking characters of "An Inspector Calls."

However, this isn't just a quote book. This guide will provide detailed analysis, based on the mark schemes for all the major GCSE exam boards. It will also offer example questions and model answers, helping you understand exactly what you need in order to gain full marks in the exam.

J.B. Priestley's "An Inspector Calls" is a gripping and thought-provoking play that continues to captivate audiences and readers alike. Set in 1912, the play revolves around the prosperous Birling family, whose comfortable and self-satisfied lives are disrupted by the sudden arrival of the mysterious Inspector Goole. Over the course of the evening, the Inspector's relentless questioning forces the family to confront their own guilt and responsibility in the death of a young working-class woman named Eva Smith.

The play is an engaging exploration of themes such as social responsibility, class, gender, and the consequences of individual actions. It is also an important social commentary, critiquing the social inequalities and hypocrisy prevalent in Edwardian society. In this guide, we will not only analyze key quotes from the text that exemplify these themes, but also examine the play's historical context and the ways in which it reflects the concerns and anxieties of post-World War II Britain.

To help you fully appreciate the depth and intricacy of Priestley's writing, this study guide also delves into the various language techniques employed throughout the play. With a focus on dramatic irony, foreshadowing, and symbolism, we will dissect the ways in which the playwright manipulates language to create tension, evoke emotions, and communicate his message. This thorough analysis of the play's literary techniques will provide you with a deeper understanding of the text, enhancing your ability to write insightful essays and engage in thought-provoking discussions.

As is required for GCSE exams, this study guide also places a strong emphasis on the historical context of "An Inspector Calls." By examining the social, political, and economic landscape of both Edwardian England and post-World War II Britain, we will delve into the ways in which the play's themes and messages are rooted in the realities and concerns of the time. This understanding of the historical context will not only enrich your interpretation of the play but also enable you to make connections between the text and the wider world.

Throughout this guide, we will also provide practical tips and strategies to help you succeed in your GCSE English Literature examination. From essay-writing techniques to tips on tackling challenging questions, this study guide will serve as a valuable resource to help you excel in your studies and achieve the best possible results.

After this guide you should know:

- A breakdown of the 100+ most important quotes from "An Inspector Calls", including language analysis and meaning.
- A complete historical context of the play including contextual analysis for every quote.
- An overview of each of the major themes from "An Inspector Calls", including the most important quotes for each.
- How to structure your essay for GCSE, including an analysis of the mark scheme and the deadly AOs.
- 25+ example essay questions, and some extremely detailed example essay answers.

2) CONTEXT

J.B. Priestley's "An Inspector Calls," written in 1945, is set in the fictional industrial town of Brumley in 1912. To fully appreciate the play, it is essential to understand its historical context and the social, political, and economic climate of both Edwardian England and post-World War II Britain.

More importantly, the major GCSE exam boards require you to mention context throughout your essay (AO3), making it very important to learn! This in-depth exploration of the historical context will provide a foundation for understanding the themes and messages of the play, enriching our interpretation of the text and its relevance to contemporary society.

This chapter will be split into two sections, the context of 1912 (when the play was set) and the context of post 1945 (when the play was first written and performed).

1. Edwardian England (1901-1914)

Named after King Edward VII, who reigned from 1901 until his death in 1910, the Edwardian era was a period of significant social, political, and economic changes in Britain. The era began with the death of Queen Victoria and ended with the outbreak of World War I in 1914.

Social Hierarchy and Class System:

Edwardian England was a highly stratified society, with a rigid class system that dictated social interactions and opportunities. The upper class, including aristocrats and wealthy businessmen like the Birlings in "An Inspector Calls," held considerable power and influence. The middle class, comprising professionals and skilled workers, aspired to attain the status and privileges of the upper class. The working class, which made up the majority of the population, often faced harsh working conditions, low wages, and limited social mobility.

Women's Rights and the Suffragette Movement:

The early 20th century witnessed an intensification of the struggle for women's rights in Britain. Women, especially those from the working and middle classes, began to challenge their limited roles in society, demanding the right to vote, better working conditions, and access to higher education. The suffragette movement, led by prominent figures like Emmeline Pankhurst, gained momentum during the Edwardian era, culminating in the Representation of the People Act in 1918, which granted voting rights to some women over the age of 30.

Labor Unrest and the Rise of Trade Unions:

The Edwardian era was marked by increased labor unrest as workers sought better wages, working conditions, and job security. Trade unions grew in strength and numbers, and strikes became more frequent and widespread. The 1911 Railway Strike and the 1912 National Miners' Strike were notable examples of workers' protests during this period. In "An Inspector Calls," the character of Eva Smith represents the plight of the working class and the consequences of industrial exploitation.

The Titanic Disaster:

On April 15, 1912, the "unsinkable" RMS Titanic struck an iceberg and sank on its maiden voyage from Southampton to New York City. More than 1,500 people lost their lives in the tragedy, which highlighted the vast disparities between the classes, as the majority of the victims were from the lower classes. Priestley's choice of setting the play in 1912, the same year as the Titanic disaster, alludes to the metaphorical "sinking" of the Edwardian class system and foreshadows the impending societal upheaval.

2. Post-World War II Britain (1945-1951)

The End of World War II:

World War II, which lasted from 1939 to 1945, had a profound impact on British society. The war resulted in the deaths of millions, including civilians, and led to widespread devastation across Europe. The collective trauma of the war led to a reassessment of societal values, particularly regarding social responsibility and the need for a more just and equal society.

The 1945 General Election and the Labour Government:

In the aftermath of World War II, Britain underwent a significant political shift. In the 1945 general election, the Labour Party, led by Clement Attlee, won a landslide victory over Winston Churchill's Conservative Party. This marked the beginning of a new era in British politics, with the Labour government focused on creating a more egalitarian society and implementing social and economic reforms.

The Welfare State and the National Health Service:

One of the most significant achievements of the post-war Labour government was the establishment of the welfare state, which aimed to provide a safety net for citizens in times of need. This included the introduction of the National Health Service (NHS) in 1948, which provided free healthcare to all British citizens, regardless of their income or social status. The establishment of the welfare state and the NHS reflected a growing sense of social responsibility and a commitment to addressing social inequalities.

The Housing Crisis and Post-War Reconstruction:

The aftermath of World War II saw a severe housing crisis in Britain, with millions of homes destroyed or damaged during the conflict. The Labour government embarked on an ambitious program of post-war reconstruction, building new homes and communities to alleviate the housing shortage. This period also witnessed the development of the modernist architectural movement, which aimed to create functional, affordable, and aesthetically pleasing living spaces for all citizens.

The Decline of the British Empire and the Rise of the Cold War:

The post-war period also saw the decline of the British Empire, as several colonies gained independence, and Britain's global influence diminished. The end of World War II marked the beginning of the Cold War, a prolonged period of political and military tension between the Western Bloc, led by the United States, and the Eastern Bloc, led by the Soviet Union. This new geopolitical landscape had far-reaching implications for British society and culture, shaping the nation's outlook and identity in the post-war years.

Connecting the Historical Context to "An Inspector Calls"

J.B. Priestley's "An Inspector Calls" is a play that masterfully intertwines the social and political concerns of both Edwardian England and post-World War II Britain. By setting the play in 1912, Priestley invites the audience to examine the flaws and injustices of Edwardian society, while simultaneously reflecting on the societal changes and aspirations of post-war Britain.

Through the character of Inspector Goole, Priestley urges the audience to recognize the importance of social responsibility and the need for a more just and equal society. The play's themes of class, gender, and individual accountability resonate with the historical context, encouraging the audience to draw connections between the text and the wider world.

Make sure you take time to read, learn, and understand the historical context of the play. Try to remember a few of the key dates, facts, and figures. If you can work some of these in your answer, particularly by relating it to the question you are asked (see the next sections), then you are well on your way to getting an excellent mark at GCSE.

3) MAIN CHARACTERS

GCSE exam questions usually focus on one of two things: Either a character, or a theme. A great way to revise involves breaking down the quotes for each major character, and breaking down the quotes for each major theme. This can help when it comes to writing your essays, as you'll have a 'bank' of quotes ready for whatever question comes up.

Also, the GCSE mark schemes require you to discuss the language of the quotes (AO2), and the context (AO3) in your answers. Therefore, for each of the characters and themes, we won't only give you the important quotes, but we will also give you some language analysis and context that you can use when discussing the quote.

Mr. Birling

1. *"The way some of these cranks talk and write now, you'd think everybody has to look after everybody else, as if we were all mixed up together like bees in a hive – community and all that nonsense."*

Meaning: Arthur Birling dismisses the idea of social responsibility and the concept of community.

Language Analysis: The simile "like bees in a hive" emphasizes Birling's disdain for collective responsibility, as it implies that people should remain separate and focus on their individual interests. The use of the word "cranks" to describe proponents of social responsibility highlights his dismissive attitude towards this perspective.

Historical Context: The quote reflects the capitalist mindset of the Edwardian era, with its emphasis on individualism and the pursuit of personal wealth.

2. *"A man has to make his own way – has to look after himself – and his family too, of course, when he has one."*

Meaning: Birling believes that a man's primary responsibility is to his family and himself, rather than the wider community.

Language Analysis: The repetition of "has to" reinforces Birling's conviction in the importance of self-reliance and individualism. The phrase "make his own way" suggests that success is achieved through personal effort rather than collective action.

Historical Context: This quote speaks to the traditional patriarchal values of the time, where men were expected to provide for their families and maintain their social status.

3. *"The Titanic – she sails next week – forty-six thousand eight hundred tons – New York in five days – and every luxury – and unsinkable, absolutely unsinkable."*

Meaning: Mr. Birling boasts about the Titanic, emphasizing its grandeur and supposed invincibility.

Language Analysis: The use of repetition and enumeration, listing the Titanic's specifications, creates a sense of awe and admiration for the ship. The phrase "absolutely unsinkable" serves as an example of dramatic irony, as the audience knows the Titanic will ultimately sink.

Historical Context: The Titanic disaster, which occurred in the same year the play is set (1912), symbolizes the hubris and arrogance of the Edwardian upper class, foreshadowing the downfall of their social order.

4. *"I'm talking as a hard-headed, practical man of business."*

Meaning: Mr. Birling emphasizes his practicality and experience as a businessman.

Language Analysis: The adjectives "hard-headed" and "practical" portray Birling as a rational, no-nonsense figure, reinforcing his self-image as a successful and knowledgeable man. This quote also exemplifies Birling's materialistic worldview.

Historical Context: This statement reflects the values of Edwardian capitalism, where business acumen and financial success were seen as indicators of a person's worth.

5. *"There'll be peace and prosperity and rapid progress everywhere."*

Meaning: Mr. Birling confidently predicts a future of peace, prosperity, and progress.

Language Analysis: The alliteration of "peace," "prosperity," and "progress" underscores Birling's optimistic outlook. This statement, however, is another instance of dramatic irony, as the audience knows that World War I and the subsequent economic turmoil are imminent.

Historical Context: This quote highlights the naïveté and complacency of the Edwardian upper class, who were unaware of the impending global conflicts and social upheavals.

6. *"Still, I can't accept any responsibility."*

Meaning: Mr. Birling refuses to acknowledge his role in Eva Smith's death.

Language Analysis: The use of the word "still" implies that despite the evidence presented by Inspector Goole, Mr. Birling remains stubbornly unwilling to change his stance. This quote demonstrates his unwillingness to accept the consequences of his actions and his persistent denial of any moral responsibility.

Historical Context: This quote speaks to the broader theme of social responsibility, which was a significant issue during the early 20th century, particularly in the context of the labor movement and workers' rights.

7. *"Lower costs and higher prices."*

Meaning: Mr. Birling describes his primary business strategy, which is to minimize expenses and maximize profits.

Language Analysis: The concise, parallel structure of "lower costs and higher prices" emphasizes Birling's focus on financial gain and his ruthless approach to business. This statement reveals his disregard for the welfare of his workers, as lower costs often meant cutting wages and reducing worker benefits.

Historical Context: This quote reflects the exploitative labor practices prevalent in Edwardian England, where business owners prioritized profits over the well-being of their employees.

8. *"You must give me a list of those accounts. I've got to cover this up as soon as I can."*

Meaning: Mr. Birling, upon discovering Eric's theft from

his business, immediately plans to cover it up to protect his reputation.

Language Analysis: The imperative "give me" and the phrase "I've got to" display Birling's urgency and determination to protect his image. This quote exposes Birling's hypocrisy and his willingness to prioritize his reputation above all else.

Historical Context: This quote highlights the corruption and moral decay present in the Edwardian upper class, which prioritized maintaining their social standing over addressing the issues of the working class.

9. "A man has to to mind his own business and look after himself and his own."

Meaning: Mr. Birling reiterates his belief in individualism and self-interest, asserting that a man should only concern himself with his own affairs and family.

Language Analysis: The repetition of "his own" emphasizes Birling's focus on self-preservation and individualism. This quote displays Birling's disregard for the welfare of others, which is central to his character and the play's themes.

Historical Context: This quote reflects the values of the Edwardian era, which prioritized self-interest and the accumulation of wealth, often at the expense of the working class.

10. *"Look, Inspector – I'd give thousands – yes, thousands."*

Meaning: Mr. Birling, desperate to avoid responsibility for Eva Smith's death, offers to pay a large sum of money to make the problem go away.

Language Analysis: The repetition of "thousands" emphasizes Birling's desperation and his reliance on wealth to solve his problems. This quote showcases his belief that money can absolve him of guilt and responsibility.

Historical Context: This quote highlights the pervasive influence of wealth in Edwardian England, where the upper class often used their financial power to evade accountability and maintain their social status.

Mrs. Birling

1. *"As if a girl of that sort would ever refuse money!"*

Meaning: Sybil Birling dismisses the notion that a working-class girl like Eva Smith would reject financial assistance.

Language Analysis: The use of "that sort" is a derogatory phrase that reflects Sybil's condescending attitude towards the lower classes. The tone of disbelief in the quote illustrates her inability to empathize with Eva's situation.

Historical Context: Sybil's statement underlines the class prejudice and social snobbery prevalent in Edwardian England, where the upper class often looked down upon those of lower social standing.

2. *"I did nothing I'm ashamed of."*

Meaning: Sybil refuses to acknowledge her responsibility in Eva Smith's death, claiming that she acted appropriately given the circumstances.

Language Analysis: The use of the word "nothing" emphasizes her denial of guilt and refusal to accept any blame. The phrase "I'm ashamed of" demonstrates her self-righteousness and inability to see the consequences of her actions.

Historical Context: This quote highlights the lack of accountability among the privileged classes in Edwardian England, who often evaded responsibility for their actions and maintained their social standing at the expense of others.

3. "I blame the young man who was the father of the child she was going to have. If, as she said, he didn't belong to her class, and was some drunken young idler, then that's all the more reason why he shouldn't escape."

Meaning: Mrs. Birling, unaware that the "young man" she is blaming is her own son, tries to deflect responsibility for Eva's death onto the unborn child's father.

Language Analysis: The use of the phrase "drunken young idler" is a derogatory characterization, which reveals her prejudice and classist attitude. The phrase "all the more reason" demonstrates her belief that the father, being of a higher social class, should be held accountable, ironically contradicting her own refusal to accept responsibility.

Historical Context: This quote reflects the class divisions and hypocrisy present in Edwardian society, where responsibility was often shifted onto others to protect one's social standing.

4.   *"He should be made an example of. If the girl's death is due to anybody, then it's due to him."*

Meaning: Mrs. Birling insists that the father of Eva's unborn child, still unaware that it's Eric, should be punished for his actions.

Language Analysis: The phrase "made an example of" reveals Mrs. Birling's desire for retribution, demonstrating her belief in punitive measures as a means of enforcing moral behavior. The use of "anybody" in the quote emphasizes her continued refusal to accept her own culpability in Eva's death.

Historical Context: This quote highlights the moral double standards present in Edwardian society, where the upper class often evaded responsibility while demanding punishment for those they deemed morally inferior.

5. *"You seem to have made a great impression on this child, Inspector."*

Meaning: Mrs. Birling condescendingly comments on the Inspector's impact on Sheila, implying that he has manipulated her emotions.

Language Analysis: The use of the word "child" to describe Sheila, an adult, reveals Mrs. Birling's patronizing attitude towards her daughter, undermining her autonomy and ability to form independent judgments.

Historical Context: This quote reflects the patriarchal norms of Edwardian society, where women were often infantilized and their opinions dismissed as emotional or irrational.

6. *"Please don't contradict me like that. And in any case, I don't suppose for a moment that we can understand why the girl committed suicide. Girls of that class—"*

Meaning: Mrs. Birling dismisses the possibility of understanding the reasons behind Eva's suicide, attributing it to her lower social class.

Language Analysis: The interruption of her own sentence with "And in any case" signals her impatience and unwillingness to consider alternative perspectives. The phrase "girls of that class" once again highlights her condescending attitude towards the working class.

Historical Context: This quote emphasizes the class divide and lack of empathy towards the working class in Edwardian society, where the upper class often failed to recognize or acknowledge the struggles faced by those in lower social strata.

7.   *"I'll tell you what I told her. Go and look for the father of the child. It's his responsibility."*

Meaning: Mrs. Birling insists that the father of Eva's unborn child should be held responsible for her situation, rather than offering help or understanding.

Language Analysis: The use of the imperative "Go" illustrates her dismissive and unyielding attitude, while the phrase "it's his responsibility" underscores her belief in assigning blame and avoiding personal accountability.

Historical Context: This quote highlights the prevailing attitudes towards women and their role in society during the Edwardian era, where women were often blamed for their own misfortunes and expected to rely on male support.

8. *"You're quite wrong to suppose I shall regret what I did."*

Meaning: Mrs. Birling maintains that she will not regret her actions, even in light of the Inspector's revelations.

Language Analysis: The phrase "quite wrong" demonstrates her unwavering certainty in her own moral righteousness, while the use of "suppose" suggests that she believes the Inspector's assumptions to be baseless and unfounded.

Historical Context: This quote highlights the obstinate refusal of the Edwardian upper class to accept responsibility for their actions or acknowledge the consequences of their decisions on others.

9. *"Yes, we've done a great deal of useful work in helping deserving cases."*

Meaning: Mrs. Birling boasts about her charitable efforts, emphasizing her role in assisting those she deems "deserving."

Language Analysis: The phrase "deserving cases" reveals her judgmental and selective approach to charity, implying that not all people in need are worthy of assistance. The use of "we" and "useful work" suggests a self-congratulatory attitude, highlighting her belief in her own benevolence.

Historical Context: This quote demonstrates the paternalistic attitudes of the Edwardian upper class towards charity, where assistance was often contingent on the recipient's perceived moral worthiness.

10. *"That – I consider – is a trifle impertinent, Inspector."*

Meaning: Mrs. Birling takes offense at the Inspector's line of questioning, believing it to be disrespectful.

Language Analysis: The use of the word "trifle" downplays the extent of her offense, suggesting a measure of restraint or an attempt to maintain an air of dignity. The phrase "I consider" asserts her authority and self-importance, emphasizing her belief that her judgment is beyond reproach.

Historical Context: This quote highlights the expectation of deference and respect afforded to the upper class in Edwardian society, where social standing and wealth often shielded individuals from criticism or accountability.

Sheila Birling

1. *"But these girls aren't cheap labor – they're people."*

Meaning: Sheila argues that the working-class girls, like Eva Smith, should be treated as human beings, not just as sources of inexpensive labor.

Language Analysis: The use of the word "people" underscores Sheila's empathy and recognition of the common humanity shared between the upper and working classes. The contrast between "cheap labor" and "people" highlights the dehumanizing nature of the capitalist system.

Historical Context: This quote reflects the growing awareness of social responsibility and workers' rights in early 20th-century England, as the labor movement gained momentum.

2. *"It's the only time I've ever done anything like that, and I'll never, never do it again to anybody."*

Meaning: Sheila expresses remorse for her actions, which contributed to Eva's dismissal from Milward's, and promises never to repeat such behavior.

Language Analysis: The repetition of "never" emphasizes her sincerity and the strength of her conviction to change her ways. This quote showcases Sheila's growth and her willingness to learn from her mistakes.

Historical Context: This quote represents a shift in attitudes towards social responsibility, as individuals began to recognize the consequences of their actions on others.

3.   *"But that won't bring Eva Smith back to life, will it?"*

Meaning: Sheila acknowledges that no amount of regret or remorse can undo the damage that has been done to Eva Smith.

Language Analysis: The use of the rhetorical question "will it?" serves to emphasize the finality of Eva's death and the irreversible nature of the consequences of the Birlings' actions.

Historical Context: This quote underscores the human cost of the social injustices and class divisions prevalent in Edwardian England.

4. *"You don't seem to have learned anything."*

Meaning: Sheila criticizes her parents for their lack of remorse and unwillingness to accept responsibility for their actions.

Language Analysis: The phrase "don't seem to" highlights Sheila's disappointment in her parents' lack of growth, while "learned anything" underscores the importance of recognizing and acknowledging one's mistakes in order to grow as individuals.

Historical Context: This quote illustrates the generational divide between the older, more conservative generation and the younger generation, who were more open to change and social progress.

5. *"I suppose we're all nice people now."*

Meaning: Sheila sarcastically comments on her family's attempt to return to normalcy after the Inspector's departure, pointing out the superficiality of their newfound "niceness."

Language Analysis: The use of the word "suppose" indicates Sheila's skepticism and disapproval, while the sarcasm in "nice people" underscores the hypocrisy and superficiality of the Birlings' self-image.

Historical Context: This quote highlights the theme of societal hypocrisy, which was prevalent in Edwardian England, where maintaining appearances was often prioritized over genuine self-improvement and social responsibility.

6.   *"You knew it was me all the time, didn't you?"*

Meaning: Sheila, feeling exposed and vulnerable, realizes that the Inspector was aware of her involvement in Eva's dismissal from the beginning.

Language Analysis: The use of the phrase "all the time" emphasizes the Inspector's omniscience and power, while "didn't you?" highlights Sheila's vulnerability and unease.

Historical Context: This quote serves to underline the Inspector's role as a moral authority and an agent of social change, challenging the Birlings' complacency and self-righteousness.

7.   *"We all started like that – so confident, so pleased with ourselves until he began asking us questions."*

Meaning: Sheila observes the transformation of her family members, who initially displayed confidence and self-assurance but began to unravel under the Inspector's questioning.

Language Analysis: The use of the contrasting phrases "so confident, so pleased with ourselves" and "until he began asking us questions" highlights the impact of the Inspector's interrogation on the Birlings' self-image and sense of security. This quote also demonstrates Sheila's growing awareness of her family's flawed moral character.

Historical Context: This quote emphasizes the power of self-examination and the need for individuals to confront their own shortcomings in order to foster personal and societal growth, a key theme in the play.

8.   *"No, he's giving us the rope – so that we'll hang ourselves."*

Meaning: Sheila suggests that the Inspector is allowing the Birlings to expose their own guilt through their words and actions.

Language Analysis: The metaphor of "giving us the rope" and "hang ourselves" symbolizes the self-destructive nature of the Birlings' attempts to evade responsibility and maintain their façade of respectability.

Historical Context: This quote highlights the play's overarching theme of moral accountability, emphasizing the importance of accepting responsibility for one's actions in order to address social injustice and inequality.

9. *"Between us we drove that girl to commit suicide."*

Meaning: Sheila acknowledges the collective responsibility of her family in Eva Smith's tragic demise, emphasizing the interconnected nature of their actions.

Language Analysis: The use of the phrase "between us" underscores the shared responsibility of the Birlings, while "we drove that girl to commit suicide" highlights the devastating consequences of their actions on Eva's life.

Historical Context: This quote reflects the growing understanding of social responsibility in the early 20th century, as individuals began to recognize the impact of their actions on the lives of others, particularly the working class.

10. *"It frightens me the way you talk."*

Meaning: Sheila expresses her fear and disbelief at her parents' inability to accept responsibility and learn from their mistakes, despite the Inspector's revelations.

Language Analysis: The phrase "it frightens me" highlights Sheila's emotional response to her parents' obstinate refusal to change, while "the way you talk" emphasizes the disconnection between their words and the reality of their actions.

Historical Context: This quote underscores the generational divide in Edwardian society, where the younger generation, represented by Sheila, began to challenge the traditional values and attitudes of their parents, pushing for a more progressive and socially responsible approach to life.

Eric Birling

1. *"You're not the kind of father a chap could go to when he's in trouble."*

Meaning: Eric expresses his frustration with his father's lack of emotional support, highlighting the distant relationship between them.

Language Analysis: The use of the word "chap" creates an informal tone, emphasizing the distance Eric feels from his father. The phrase "when he's in trouble" underlines the absence of emotional support Eric receives from Mr. Birling.

Historical Context: This quote reflects the rigid expectations and emotional distance often found in parent-child relationships in Edwardian society, particularly between fathers and sons.

2. *"And I say the girl's dead and we all helped to kill her – and that's what matters."*

Meaning: Eric asserts that the Birlings are collectively responsible for Eva Smith's death, emphasizing the importance of acknowledging their role in the tragedy.

Language Analysis: The repetition of "and" creates a sense of urgency, underscoring the weight of their actions. The phrase "that's what matters" demonstrates Eric's commitment to accepting responsibility and addressing the consequences of their actions.

Historical Context: This quote highlights the theme of collective responsibility and the need for individuals to confront their own moral shortcomings in order to address social injustice and inequality.

3.   *"I was in that state when a chap easily turns nasty."*

Meaning: Eric admits that his intoxication led him to behave aggressively towards Eva Smith, revealing his regret for his actions.

Language Analysis: The phrase "that state" refers to Eric's drunkenness, while "easily turns nasty" conveys the ease with which he behaved aggressively. This acknowledgment highlights Eric's self-awareness and willingness to confront his mistakes.

Historical Context: This quote exposes the darker side of Edwardian society, where alcoholism and aggressive behavior were often hidden behind a façade of respectability.

4. *"I don't even remember – that's the hellish thing."*

Meaning: Eric laments his inability to recall his actions due to his intoxicated state, emphasizing his guilt and remorse.

Language Analysis: The use of the word "hellish" intensifies the emotional weight of his regret, while "don't even remember" highlights the destructive nature of alcohol abuse and the consequences of his actions.

Historical Context: This quote provides a glimpse into the moral decay of Edwardian society, where excessive alcohol consumption often led to destructive behavior and devastating consequences for those involved.

5. *"You lot may be letting yourselves out nicely, but I can't."*

Meaning: Eric criticizes his family's attempts to avoid responsibility for their actions, expressing his own commitment to accepting accountability.

Language Analysis: The use of the phrase "you lot" distances Eric from the rest of his family, demonstrating his disapproval of their behavior. The word "nicely" conveys a sense of sarcasm, highlighting the superficiality and hypocrisy of their attempts to evade responsibility.

Historical Context: This quote underscores the generational divide of the time, where younger characters like Eric begin to challenge the traditional values and attitudes of their parents, pushing for a more progressive and socially responsible approach to life. This was a time of change in England, and language like this certainly reflects that.

6. *"The fact remains that I did what I did."*

Meaning: Eric acknowledges his actions and their consequences, accepting responsibility for his role in Eva Smith's tragic fate.

Language Analysis: The phrase "fact remains" emphasizes the immutable nature of his actions and their consequences, while "I did what I did" demonstrates his willingness to confront his mistakes and take responsibility for them.

Historical Context: This quote highlights the theme of moral accountability, emphasizing the importance of accepting responsibility for one's actions in order to address social injustice and inequality.

7. *"My God – I'm not likely to forget."*

Meaning: Eric expresses his deep remorse for his actions and the consequences they had on Eva Smith, emphasizing that he will never forget what he has done.

Language Analysis: The use of the exclamation "My God" conveys the intensity of Eric's emotions, while "I'm not likely to forget" underscores his commitment to learning from his mistakes and remembering the impact of his actions.

Historical Context: This quote demonstrates a shift in attitudes towards social responsibility, as individuals like Eric begin to recognize the consequences of their actions on the lives of others, particularly the working class.

8. *"She was pretty and a good sport."*

Meaning: Eric describes Eva Smith in a positive light, highlighting her attractiveness and her enjoyable company.

Language Analysis: The phrase "pretty and a good sport" offers a glimpse into Eric's attraction to Eva, as well as his appreciation for her personality. However, it also reveals the superficial nature of their relationship, as he focuses on her physical appearance and her ability to provide entertainment.

Historical Context: This quote offers insight into the objectification and mistreatment of working-class women during the Edwardian era, who were often seen as disposable sources of pleasure for men in higher social strata.

9. *"You're beginning to pretend now that nothing's really happened at all."*

Meaning: Eric criticizes his family's attempts to ignore the consequences of their actions, accusing them of denial and hypocrisy.

Language Analysis: The use of the phrase "beginning to pretend" highlights the superficial nature of the Birlings' attempts to evade responsibility, while "nothing's really happened at all" underscores the stark contrast between their denial and the reality of their actions.

Historical Context: This quote emphasizes the theme of

societal hypocrisy, which was prevalent in Edwardian England, where maintaining appearances was often prioritized over genuine self-improvement and social responsibility.

10. *"The money's not the important thing. It's what happened to the girl and what we all did to her that matters."*

Meaning: Eric asserts that financial compensation cannot absolve the Birlings of their responsibility for Eva Smith's death, emphasizing the importance of acknowledging their actions and their consequences.

Language Analysis: The contrast between "money" and "what happened to the girl" highlights the insufficiency of material reparations in addressing moral responsibility.

Historical Context: This quote reflects the growing understanding of social responsibility in the early 20th century, as individuals began to recognize the impact of their actions on the lives of others and the need for genuine accountability and change in order to address social injustice and inequality.

Gerald

1. *"I didn't feel about her as she felt about me."*

Meaning: Gerald admits that his feelings for Eva Smith were not as deep as her feelings for him, highlighting the imbalance in their relationship.

Language Analysis: The contrast between "I didn't feel" and "as she felt" emphasizes the emotional disparity between Gerald and Eva, reflecting the unequal power dynamics in their relationship.

Historical Context: This quote offers insight into the casual relationships between upper-class men and working-class women during the Edwardian era, revealing the lack of emotional investment from the men involved.

2. *"I'm rather more – upset – by this business than I probably appear to be."*

Meaning: Gerald reveals that he is more emotionally affected by Eva Smith's death than he outwardly shows, hinting at his inner turmoil.

Language Analysis: The use of the word "upset" combined with the hesitation in Gerald's speech, marked by the dashes, conveys his struggle to express his emotions and the depth of his feelings about the situation.

Historical Context: This quote reflects the societal expectations placed on men in the Edwardian era to maintain a stoic façade and hide their emotions, even when faced with tragedy.

3. *"That's when it happened – and I don't suppose for a moment that we can understand why."*

Meaning: Gerald acknowledges the difficulty in comprehending the reasons behind Eva Smith's suicide, recognizing the complexity of her emotional state.

Language Analysis: The use of the phrase "when it happened" refers to Eva's suicide, while "we can understand why" highlights the impossibility of truly grasping her emotional turmoil. This demonstrates Gerald's awareness of the limits of his own understanding.

Historical Context: This quote underlines the theme of social responsibility, as it underscores the need for empathy and compassion towards those who are less fortunate and acknowledges the difficulties faced by the working class in Edwardian England.

4. *"Everything's all right now, Sheila. What about this ring?"*

Meaning: After the Inspector's departure, Gerald attempts to return to normalcy by offering Sheila her engagement ring back, as if nothing has happened.

Language Analysis: The phrase "everything's all right now" conveys Gerald's desire to put the Inspector's visit behind them, while "what about this ring?" emphasizes the superficial nature of his attempt to repair their relationship.

Historical Context: This quote demonstrates the reluctance of some individuals in Edwardian society to confront their moral shortcomings and learn from their mistakes, preferring instead to maintain appearances and superficial relationships.

5. *"You know, I've been thinking that she didn't really belong to our set – to our class of life."*

Meaning: Gerald expresses his belief that Eva Smith was different from the people in their social circle, suggesting a divide between classes.

Language Analysis: The repetitive phrases "our set" and "our class of life" emphasize the social distinctions that separated the Birlings from Eva Smith, while "didn't really belong" suggests her exclusion from their privileged world.

Historical Context: This quote highlights the rigid class distinctions that defined Edwardian society, where individuals were often judged and categorized based on their social status, limiting opportunities for social mobility and reinforcing inequality.

6. *"I hate those hard-eyed dough-faced women."*

Meaning: Gerald expresses his dislike for women who lack warmth and genuine emotion, possibly alluding to the women in his social circle.

Language Analysis: The use of the phrases "hard-eyed" and "dough-faced" convey a sense of coldness and artificiality, emphasizing Gerald's preference for more authentic and genuine connections.

Historical Context: This quote reflects the superficiality of relationships within the upper-class circles of

Edwardian society, where appearance and social status often took precedence over genuine emotional connections.

7. *"We're respectable citizens and not dangerous criminals."*

Meaning: Gerald tries to downplay the Birlings' responsibility for Eva Smith's death, suggesting that their actions were not criminal in nature.

Language Analysis: The contrast between "respectable citizens" and "dangerous criminals" emphasizes Gerald's attempt to distance the Birlings from any wrongdoing and maintain their social standing.

Historical Context: This quote underscores the theme of societal hypocrisy in Edwardian England, where maintaining appearances and social respectability were often prioritized over acknowledging and addressing moral shortcomings.

8. *"I insisted on a parting gift of enough money to see her through the end of the year."*

Meaning: Gerald reveals that he provided financial assistance to Eva Smith before ending their relationship, indicating some sense of responsibility and care for her wellbeing.

Language Analysis: The use of the phrase "parting gift" conveys a sense of generosity and compassion, while "enough money to see her through the end of the year" suggests an attempt to alleviate her financial struggles.

Historical Context: This quote offers a glimpse into the power dynamics of relationships between the upper and working classes in Edwardian society, where financial assistance could be used as a means to maintain control or ease guilt.

9.   *"You're the one I feel sorry for."*

Meaning: Gerald expresses sympathy for Sheila, acknowledging the impact of the Inspector's visit on her emotions and beliefs.

Language Analysis: The phrase "the one I feel sorry for" conveys a sense of genuine concern and empathy, emphasizing the emotional connection between Gerald and Sheila, despite their earlier disagreements.

Historical Context: This quote highlights the generational divide in Edwardian society, where younger characters like Sheila and Gerald begin to question the values and attitudes of their parents, pushing for a more progressive and socially responsible approach to life.

10. *"We've been had, that's all."*

Meaning: Gerald suggests that the Inspector's visit was a hoax designed to manipulate the Birlings, downplaying the significance of the events that transpired.

Language Analysis: The phrase "we've been had" conveys a sense of trickery and deception, while "that's all" minimizes the importance of the moral lessons imparted by the Inspector's visit.

Historical Context: This quote illustrates the reluctance of some characters to acknowledge their moral responsibility for the consequences of their actions, preferring to see themselves as victims of manipulation rather than confronting the reality of their role in Eva Smith's tragic fate.

The Inspector

1. *"We don't live alone. We are members of one body. We are responsible for each other."*

Meaning: The Inspector emphasizes the interconnectedness of humanity and the importance of social responsibility.

Language Analysis: The repetition of "we" creates a sense of unity and shared responsibility, while "members of one body" uses a metaphor to convey the idea that individual actions affect the collective whole.

Historical Context: This quote reflects the growing awareness of social responsibility in the early 20th century, in response to the class divide and social inequality present in Edwardian England.

2. *"Each of you helped to kill her. Remember that. Never forget it."*

Meaning: The Inspector holds each of the Birlings accountable for Eva Smith's death, urging them to learn from their mistakes and remember the consequences of their actions.

Language Analysis: The use of the imperative verbs "remember" and "never forget" highlights the importance of acknowledging one's responsibility, while "each of you helped to kill her" underscores the collective guilt shared by the characters.

Historical Context: The quote exemplifies the theme of social responsibility, promoting self-reflection and accountability for one's actions within the broader context of societal change and progress.

3. *"Public men, Mr. Birling, have responsibilities as well as privileges."*

Meaning: The Inspector reminds Mr. Birling that people in positions of power must be mindful of their social responsibilities, not just their personal benefits.

Language Analysis: The contrast between "responsibilities" and "privileges" emphasizes the need for balance and consideration of the greater good in exercising power and influence.

Historical Context: This statement reflects the changing attitudes towards the role of the upper class in

Edwardian society, with an increasing emphasis on empathy and social responsibility towards the working class.

4. *"It's better to ask for the earth than to take it."*

Meaning: The Inspector suggests that it is better to request or negotiate fairly for resources and opportunities, rather than forcefully or selfishly taking them without considering the consequences.

Language Analysis: The use of the metaphor "ask for the earth" represents the desire for material possessions and opportunities, while "take it" implies the act of exploiting others for personal gain.

Historical Context: This quote highlights the need for a more equitable and just society, challenging the exploitative practices that were common in Edwardian England.

5. *"If men will not learn that lesson, then they will be taught it in fire and blood and anguish."*

Meaning: The Inspector warns that if people do not

learn the importance of social responsibility, they will face devastating consequences.

Language Analysis: The use of the vivid and powerful imagery in "fire and blood and anguish" emphasizes the dire consequences of failing to learn and practice social responsibility.

Historical Context: This quote foreshadows the world wars and the resulting societal upheaval, which would force people to confront the importance of empathy, cooperation, and social responsibility.

6. *"One Eva Smith has gone – but there are millions and millions of Eva Smiths and John Smiths still left with us."*

Meaning: The Inspector emphasizes that Eva Smith's story is not unique, and countless others continue to face similar struggles and injustices.

Language Analysis: The repetition of "millions and millions" stresses the magnitude of the issue, while the use of "Eva Smiths and John Smiths" represents the universality of the working class's struggles.

Historical Context: This quote speaks to the broader issues of social inequality and class struggle in Edwardian society, urging the audience to consider the impact of their actions on the lives of the less fortunate.

7. *"You see, we have to share something. If there's nothing else, we'll have to share our guilt."*

Meaning: The Inspector highlights that the Birlings cannot escape their shared guilt and responsibility for Eva Smith's death.

Language Analysis: The use of "we have to share something" implies a sense of inevitability, while "share our guilt" emphasizes the collective nature of responsibility and accountability.

Historical Context: This quote underscores the theme of social responsibility, urging the characters and the audience to recognize their shared culpability in perpetuating societal inequality and injustice.

8. *"I tell you that the time will soon come when, if men will not learn that lesson, they will be taught it in fire and blood and anguish."*

Meaning: The Inspector reiterates his warning about the consequences of failing to learn the importance of social responsibility.

Language Analysis: The repetition of "fire and blood and anguish" serves to reinforce the severity of the consequences, while the conditional phrase "if men will not learn" emphasizes the choice individuals have to change their ways.

Historical Context: This quote can be seen as a reference to the world wars, which forced societies to confront the destructive consequences of selfishness, greed, and a lack of empathy.

9. *"She was here alone, friendless, almost penniless, desperate."*

Meaning: The Inspector describes Eva Smith's desperate situation, emphasizing the vulnerability of those in the working class.

Language Analysis: The use of the adjectives "alone," "friendless," "penniless," and "desperate" creates a vivid and poignant image of Eva's suffering, evoking sympathy and empathy from the audience.

Historical Context: This quote highlights the harsh realities faced by many working-class individuals in Edwardian England, where opportunities for social mobility were limited and support systems were often lacking.

10. *"You must remember that a chain of events could have been started by just one person."*

Meaning: The Inspector explains the domino effect of individual actions, emphasizing that each person's choices can have far-reaching consequences.

Language Analysis: The metaphor of a "chain of events" demonstrates the interconnectedness of actions and consequences, while "just one person" emphasizes the importance of personal responsibility.

Historical Context: This quote ties in with the theme of social responsibility, urging individuals to consider the impact of their actions on others and the broader society. The idea of a "chain of events" resonates with the audience, as it demonstrates the interconnectedness of actions in a rapidly changing world.

4) MAIN THEMES

"An Inspector Calls" explores several key themes relevant to both its historical context and the modern world. For GCSE students, understanding these themes is crucial in order to analyze the play effectively. Exam questions will often be on a specific theme, so it's important to know each of the major themes and some significant quotes for each.

Some of the main themes in "An Inspector Calls" include:

1. **Social Responsibility**: One of the central themes in the play is the idea that individuals have a responsibility to care for and support one another. The Inspector's investigation reveals how each character's actions contributed to Eva Smith's tragic fate, emphasizing the importance

of considering the consequences of one's actions on others.

2. **Class and Social Inequality**: The play explores the vast differences between the upper and working classes in Edwardian England. Eva Smith's story highlights the struggles faced by the working class, while the Birlings represent the privileged upper class. The play examines the ways in which the upper class exploits and oppresses the working class, and the need for greater empathy and understanding between social classes.

3. **Generational Divide**: "An Inspector Calls" highlights the differing attitudes and values between the older and younger generations. The younger characters, Sheila and Eric, display a willingness to learn from their mistakes and change their behavior, while the older characters, Mr. and Mrs. Birling, remain stubborn and resistant to change. This theme suggests that progress and social change may be more achievable through the younger generation.

4. **Guilt and Responsibility**: Throughout the play, the characters are confronted with their guilt and responsibility for Eva Smith's death. The Inspector's questioning forces them to face their actions and consider the consequences they had on another person's life. The differing reactions to this guilt highlight the characters' moral compass and willingness to accept responsibility for their actions.

5. **Power and Authority**: The play examines the dynamics of power and authority, both in terms of the Inspector's role and the social hierarchy. The Birlings, as members of the upper class, wield significant power and influence over the working class, but the Inspector challenges their authority and forces them to face the consequences of their actions.

Here are some of the top quotes for each of the themes. **Some of these quotes will be the same as listed in the character section**, but we will list them again as they are also relevant for theme questions, and the language/context analysis is also slightly different in this section, focusing more on the specific theme itself.

Plus, in case you were thinking of forgetting them, perhaps listing them again will help you remember!

Social Responsibility

1. *"A man has to mind his own business and look after himself and his own."*

Meaning: Mr. Birling expresses his belief in individualism and self-preservation, dismissing the idea of social responsibility.

Language Analysis: The repetition of "his own" emphasizes Mr. Birling's focus on personal gain and individualism, in stark contrast to the Inspector's message of interconnectedness and collective responsibility.

Historical Context: This quote reflects the prevalent capitalist mindset of Edwardian England, where individual success was often prioritized over the welfare of others, perpetuating social inequality.

2. *"These girls aren't cheap labor – they're people."*

Meaning: Sheila argues against the exploitation of the working class, recognizing their humanity and inherent value.

Language Analysis: The contrast between "cheap labor" and "people" highlights the dehumanizing effect of exploitative labor practices and emphasizes the need for empathy and compassion in addressing social inequality.

Historical Context: Sheila's statement challenges the prevailing attitudes of her time, advocating for workers' rights and fair treatment, foreshadowing the labor movement and workers' rights activism in the 20th century.

3. *"We are all members of one body."*

Meaning: The Inspector emphasizes the interconnectedness of society and the importance of considering the impact of one's actions on others.

Language Analysis: The metaphor of "one body" conveys the idea that individual actions affect the collective whole, reinforcing the play's central theme of social responsibility.

Historical Context: This quote captures the growing awareness of social responsibility and the need for empathy in early 20th century England, as the nation grappled with widespread social inequality.

4. *"It's my duty to ask questions."*

Meaning: The Inspector explains that it is his responsibility to uncover the truth and hold individuals accountable for their actions.

Language Analysis: The use of the word "duty" suggests a moral obligation to pursue justice and encourage self-reflection, aligning with the play's theme of social responsibility.

Historical Context: The Inspector's role as an agent of moral accountability resonates with the social and political changes occurring in the early 20th century, as society began to question traditional power structures and advocate for greater social responsibility.

5. *"You lot may be letting yourselves out nicely, but I can't."*

Meaning: Eric expresses his unwillingness to absolve himself of guilt and responsibility for Eva Smith's death.

Language Analysis: The phrase "letting yourselves out nicely" conveys the idea of avoiding responsibility or moral accountability, while "I can't" underscores Eric's commitment to confronting the consequences of his actions.

Historical Context: Eric's statement reflects the generational divide in attitudes towards social responsibility, as younger characters like Eric and Sheila demonstrate a willingness to accept responsibility and advocate for change.

6. "We've no excuse now for putting on airs."

Meaning: Sheila acknowledges that the Birlings' superficial respectability has been shattered by the revelations of the Inspector's investigation.

Language Analysis: The phrase "putting on airs" suggests the pretense of social superiority, emphasizing the need for genuine empathy and compassion rather than maintaining a facade of respectability.

Historical Context: This quote challenges the societal values of Edwardian England, where maintaining appearances and social respectability were often prioritized over genuine moral character and social responsibility.

7. *"You don't seem to have learned anything."*

Meaning: Sheila expresses her disappointment in her parents' unwillingness to accept responsibility for their actions and learn from their mistakes.

Language Analysis: The use of "learned anything" highlights the educational aspect of the Inspector's visit and the importance of self-reflection in embracing social responsibility.

Historical Context: Sheila's statement underscores the generational divide between the older and younger characters, reflecting the changing attitudes towards social responsibility and the hope for a more empathetic and just society in the future.

8. *"You began to learn something. And now you've stopped."*

Meaning: The Inspector comments on the characters' initial willingness to learn from their mistakes but criticizes their eventual dismissal of responsibility.

Language Analysis: The contrast between "began to learn" and "now you've stopped" emphasizes the fleeting nature of the characters' self-reflection and underscores the importance of maintaining a commitment to social responsibility.

Historical Context: This quote highlights the challenge of sustaining genuine moral growth and social change in a society resistant to accepting responsibility for its actions, reflecting the broader struggle for social justice in early 20th century England.

9. *"We don't live alone. We are members of one body. We are responsible for each other."*

Meaning: The Inspector reiterates the central theme of social responsibility, emphasizing the interconnectedness of individuals within society.

Language Analysis: The repetition of "we" highlights the collective nature of responsibility, while the metaphor of "one body" reinforces the idea that individual actions have far-reaching consequences.

Historical Context: This quote captures the growing awareness of social responsibility and interconnectedness in early 20th century England, as the nation confronted the devastating effects of social inequality and sought to promote a more equitable and compassionate society.

10. *"You'll be able to divide the responsibility between you when I've gone."*

Meaning: The Inspector suggests that the characters must confront their shared responsibility for Eva Smith's death after he leaves.

Language Analysis: The phrase "divide the responsibility" conveys the idea of shared culpability and the need for collective self-reflection and accountability.

Historical Context: This quote reinforces the theme of social responsibility, reminding both the characters and the audience of the importance of acknowledging and addressing the consequences of their actions on others and the broader society.

Class & Social Inequality

1. *"Lower costs and higher prices."*

Meaning: Mr. Birling is discussing his business strategy, which involves reducing expenses and increasing profits, often at the expense of his workers.

Language Analysis: This concise phrase captures the essence of capitalist thinking, prioritizing financial gain over the welfare of the workers, contributing to social inequality.

Historical Context: This quote reflects the capitalist mindset of Edwardian England, where business owners often exploited their workers to maximize profits, perpetuating class divisions and social inequality.

2. *"She'd had a lot to say – far too much – so she had to go."*

Meaning: Mr. Birling justifies firing Eva Smith for demanding better wages, showing his disregard for the working class's struggles.

Language Analysis: The use of "far too much" implies that Eva's demands were excessive or inappropriate, while "she had to go" highlights Mr. Birling's authoritarian attitude towards his workers.

Historical Context: This quote exemplifies the power dynamics between the upper and working classes in Edwardian England, where workers often faced dismissal for advocating for better working conditions.

3. *"As if a girl of that sort would ever refuse money!"*

Meaning: Mrs. Birling expresses her disbelief that Eva Smith would refuse financial help, revealing her condescending attitude towards the working class.

Language Analysis: The phrase "a girl of that sort" demonstrates Mrs. Birling's prejudiced view of the working class, assuming that they would prioritize money over self-respect.

Historical Context: This quote highlights the class-based prejudices prevalent in Edwardian England, where the upper class often viewed the working class as morally inferior or desperate.

4. *"I don't come into this suicide business."*

Meaning: Mr. Birling tries to distance himself from Eva Smith's death, refusing to accept responsibility for her plight.

Language Analysis: The phrase "suicide business" trivializes Eva's death and suggests that Mr. Birling views the situation as unrelated to him, reflecting his disregard for the working class's struggles.

Historical Context: This quote showcases the attitude of some upper-class individuals during the Edwardian era, who felt little or no responsibility for the suffering of those in lower social classes.

5.   *"You were the wonderful Fairy Prince."*

Meaning: Sheila sarcastically addresses Gerald after learning about his affair with Eva Smith, highlighting the power dynamics between men and vulnerable working-class women.

Language Analysis: The use of "Fairy Prince" as a sarcastic title illustrates the disparity between Gerald's privileged position and Eva's vulnerable status.

Historical Context: This quote sheds light on the issue of gender and class dynamics in Edwardian England, where upper-class men often took advantage of working-class women.

6. *"I don't suppose for a moment that we can understand why the girl committed suicide."*

Meaning: Mrs. Birling dismisses the possibility of understanding Eva's reasons for suicide, revealing her lack of empathy for the working class.

Language Analysis: The phrase "I don't suppose for a moment" suggests that Mrs. Birling is not even willing to entertain the idea of understanding Eva's perspective, reflecting her class-based prejudice and lack of empathy.

Historical Context: This quote highlights the disconnect between the upper and working classes in Edwardian England, where the privileged class often failed to understand or empathize with the struggles of those less fortunate.

7. *"We've done a great deal of useful work in helping deserving cases."*

Meaning: Mrs. Birling boasts about her charity work, showcasing her belief in selectively helping those she deems "deserving."

Language Analysis: The term "deserving cases" implies a subjective judgment, suggesting that Mrs. Birling feels qualified to determine who is deserving of help, perpetuating class-based prejudice.

Historical Context: This quote reflects the paternalistic attitudes of the upper class in Edwardian England, who often engaged in charity work as a way to maintain their sense of moral superiority.

8. *"It's better to ask for the Earth than to take it."*

Meaning: The Inspector criticizes the Birlings' entitlement and exploitation of the working class, arguing that it is better to ask for help than to take advantage of others.

Language Analysis: The metaphor of "asking for the Earth" conveys the idea of making excessive demands, while "to take it" highlights the exploitative nature of the Birlings' actions.

Historical Context: This quote comments on the power dynamics and social inequality of the Edwardian era, advocating for a more equitable and empathetic society that values the welfare of all its members.

9. *"If men will not learn that lesson, then they will be taught it in fire and blood and anguish."*

Meaning: The Inspector delivers a grave warning, suggesting that if people do not learn to care for each other and address social inequality, they will face dire consequences.

Language Analysis: The use of "fire and blood and anguish" creates a vivid and dramatic image, emphasizing the severity of the consequences if society fails to address social inequality and embrace empathy.

Historical Context: This quote foreshadows the social upheaval and world conflicts that would follow in the 20th century, highlighting the urgent need for social change and a greater sense of responsibility for the well-being of others, regardless of their social class.

Generational Divide

1. *"You're beginning to pretend now that nothing's really happened at all."*

Meaning: Sheila confronts her parents for trying to dismiss the Inspector's revelations and maintain their innocence.

Language Analysis: The use of "pretend" suggests that the older generation is choosing to ignore the truth, while "nothing's really happened" emphasizes their denial of responsibility.

Historical Context: This quote highlights the generational divide in attitudes towards social responsibility, with younger characters like Sheila more willing to accept responsibility and advocate for change.

2. *"It's what happened to the girl and what we all did to her that matters."*

Meaning: Eric emphasizes the importance of recognizing the consequences of their actions on Eva Smith, rather than focusing on maintaining their reputation.

Language Analysis: The phrase "what we all did to her" highlights the collective responsibility of the characters, contrasting with the older generation's focus on individualism and self-preservation.

Historical Context: This quote reflects the growing awareness of social responsibility among the younger generation in early 20th century England, as they challenge the traditional values of their parents.

3. *"You don't understand anything. You never did. You never even tried."*

Meaning: Sheila accuses her mother of failing to comprehend the gravity of the situation and the importance of acknowledging their responsibility.

Language Analysis: The repetition of "never" underscores the persistent lack of understanding and empathy displayed by the older generation.

Historical Context: This quote highlights the generational divide in attitudes towards empathy and social responsibility, as younger characters challenge the moral shortcomings of their parents.

4.   *"The famous younger generation who know it
all. And they can't even take a joke."*

Meaning: Mr. Birling mocks the younger generation's
perceived arrogance and inability to understand humor,
dismissing their concerns as overreactions.

Language Analysis: The use of "famous" sarcastically
highlights Mr. Birling's disdain for the younger
generation's moral stance, while "can't even take a
joke" trivializes their concerns.

Historical Context: This quote captures the tension
between the older and younger generations, as they
navigate the changing societal values and expectations
of early 20th century England.

5.   *"You mustn't try to build up a kind of wall
between us and that girl."*

Meaning: Sheila urges her parents not to distance
themselves from their responsibility towards Eva Smith
and the working class.

Language Analysis: The metaphor of "a kind of wall"
illustrates the emotional and moral barriers the older
generation attempts to construct to avoid facing their

guilt.

Historical Context: This quote highlights the generational divide in attitudes towards social responsibility, with younger characters like Sheila advocating for empathy and accountability.

6. *"I know I'm to blame – and I'm desperately sorry."*

Meaning: Eric accepts his responsibility for his actions and demonstrates genuine remorse for his role in Eva Smith's death.

Language Analysis: The use of "desperately sorry" conveys the depth of Eric's regret and contrasts with the older generation's attempts to avoid responsibility.

Historical Context: Eric's statement reflects the generational shift in attitudes towards empathy and social responsibility, as the younger generation embraces self-reflection and moral growth.

7. *"There'll be plenty of time, when I've gone, for you all to adjust your family relationships."*

Meaning: The Inspector suggests that the Birlings will need to address their internal conflicts and generational differences after his departure.

Language Analysis: The phrase "adjust your family relationships" implies that the Birlings must confront the generational divide and reassess their values.

Historical Context: This quote emphasizes the need for both personal and societal change in early 20th century England, as families grapple with the evolving values and expectations of younger generations.

8.   *"You don't seem to have learned anything."*

Meaning: Sheila expresses her frustration with her parents' refusal to accept responsibility and learn from their mistakes.

Language Analysis: The phrase "don't seem to have learned anything" highlights the older generation's stubbornness and reluctance to embrace change or self-reflection.

Historical Context: This quote underscores the generational divide in attitudes towards moral growth and social responsibility, as younger characters challenge the older generation's refusal to acknowledge their culpability.

9.   *"Everything to lose and nothing to gain by war."*

Meaning: Mr. Birling expresses his belief in the unlikelihood of war, reflecting the complacency and naivety of the older generation.

Language Analysis: The contrast between "everything to lose" and "nothing to gain" highlights Mr. Birling's belief in the stability of the existing social order, which the younger generation challenges.

Historical Context: This quote demonstrates the generational divide in perspectives on social change and global conflicts, as the older generation clings to outdated notions of peace and stability while the younger generation confronts the harsh realities of a rapidly changing world.

Guilt & Responsibility

1. *"I wasn't in love with her or anything – but I liked her – she was pretty and a good sport."*

Meaning: Eric admits to having a casual relationship with Eva Smith, acknowledging his role in her tragic circumstances.

Language Analysis: The use of "pretty" and "a good sport" underscores the superficial nature of Eric's relationship with Eva, revealing his lack of genuine emotional investment and highlighting his moral shortcomings.

Historical Context: This quote exposes the exploitative relationships between the upper and working classes in Edwardian England, as well as the growing awareness of social responsibility among the younger generation.

2. *"It's my duty to ask questions."*

Meaning: The Inspector asserts his responsibility to investigate the Birlings' actions and uncover the truth about Eva Smith's death.

Language Analysis: The use of "duty" emphasizes the Inspector's commitment to justice and his role as a moral authority, challenging the Birlings' sense of entitlement and self-interest.

Historical Context: This quote reflects the growing demand for accountability and social responsibility in early 20th century England, as society grapples with the consequences of social inequality and moral corruption.

3. *"You see, we have to share something. If there's nothing else, we'll have to share our guilt."*

Meaning: The Inspector stresses the need for the Birlings to acknowledge their collective guilt and responsibility for Eva Smith's death.

Language Analysis: The repetition of "share" emphasizes the interconnectedness of the characters and the importance of recognizing their shared culpability.

Historical Context: This quote highlights the growing awareness of social responsibility and interconnectedness in early 20th century England, as individuals are called to confront the consequences of their actions on others.

4. *"You lot may be letting yourselves out nicely, but I can't."*

Meaning: Sheila admits her guilt and refuses to let herself off the hook, unlike her parents who are more focused on preserving their reputations.

Language Analysis: The phrase "letting yourselves out nicely" highlights the older generation's attempts to evade responsibility, contrasting with Sheila's determination to face the consequences of her actions.

Historical Context: This quote illustrates the generational divide in attitudes towards guilt and responsibility, with younger characters like Sheila embracing self-reflection and moral growth.

5. *"I'm ashamed of you."*

Meaning: Sheila expresses her disappointment with her parents' refusal to accept responsibility for their actions and learn from their mistakes.

Language Analysis: The use of "ashamed" underscores Sheila's emotional reaction to her parents' behavior, highlighting the generational divide in attitudes towards guilt and responsibility.

Historical Context: This quote captures the growing tension between the older and younger generations in early 20th century England, as they navigate the evolving values and expectations surrounding social responsibility and moral growth.

6.   *"We don't live alone. We are members of one body. We are responsible for each other."*

Meaning: The Inspector emphasizes the interconnectedness of society and the importance of recognizing our collective responsibility towards one another.

Language Analysis: The metaphor of "one body" illustrates the idea that everyone's actions impact others, stressing the need for empathy and social responsibility.

Historical Context: This quote reflects the growing awareness of social responsibility and interconnectedness in early 20th century England, as individuals confront the consequences of their actions on the wider community.

7. *"You'll be able to divide the factory into two halves – you'll be living in one half and working in the other."*

Meaning: Mr. Birling describes the division between the Birlings' personal and professional lives, suggesting that they can compartmentalize their guilt and responsibility.

Language Analysis: The imagery of "divide the factory into two halves" symbolizes the separation of personal and professional spheres, highlighting the Birlings' attempts to evade responsibility for their actions.

Historical Context: This quote illustrates the shifting attitudes towards guilt and responsibility in early 20th century England, as the younger generation challenges the older generation's attempts to distance themselves from the consequences of their actions.

8. *"You began to learn something. And now you've stopped."*

Meaning: The Inspector criticizes the Birlings for failing to learn from their mistakes and accept responsibility for their actions.

Language Analysis: The contrast between "began to learn" and "now you've stopped" underscores the Birlings' reluctance to embrace self-reflection and moral growth, highlighting the generational divide in attitudes towards guilt and responsibility.

Historical Context: This quote captures the ongoing struggle for moral growth and social responsibility in early 20th century England, as individuals are called to confront the consequences of their actions and learn from their mistakes.

Power & Authority

1. *"A man has to make his own way – has to look after himself – and his family too, of course, when he has one."*

Meaning: Mr. Birling advocates for individualism and self-reliance, asserting his belief in the importance of personal power and authority.

Language Analysis: The repetition of "has to" emphasizes Mr. Birling's belief in the necessity of pursuing personal success and maintaining control over one's own life.

Historical Context: This quote reflects the traditional values of early 20th century England, where individualism and self-reliance were highly prized, particularly among the upper classes.

2. *"Public men, Mr. Birling, have responsibilities as well as privileges."*

Meaning: The Inspector reminds Mr. Birling of the

responsibilities that come with power and authority, challenging his sense of entitlement.

Language Analysis: The juxtaposition of "responsibilities" and "privileges" highlights the Inspector's message that power should be used responsibly and not solely for personal gain.

Historical Context: This quote speaks to the growing awareness of social responsibility in early 20th century England, as people began to question the actions and motives of those in positions of power.

3. *"I don't play golf."*

Meaning: The Inspector rejects Mr. Birling's attempt to establish a connection based on shared interests, asserting his independence and authority.

Language Analysis: The blunt statement "I don't play golf" underscores the Inspector's refusal to engage in superficial camaraderie, emphasizing his focus on the task at hand.

Historical Context: This quote highlights the tension between the traditional values of camaraderie and social connections and the emerging focus on social responsibility and justice in early 20th century England.

4. *"I'm on duty, Mr. Birling."*

Meaning: The Inspector asserts his authority as a police officer, reminding Mr. Birling of his professional obligations.

Language Analysis: The use of "duty" emphasizes the Inspector's commitment to his role as a moral authority, challenging Mr. Birling's sense of entitlement and self-importance.

Historical Context: This quote reflects the growing demand for accountability and justice in early 20th century England, as individuals in positions of power were increasingly called to answer for their actions.

5. *"There are millions and millions of Eva Smiths and John Smiths still left with us."*

Meaning: The Inspector uses the metaphor of "Eva Smiths and John Smiths" to represent the countless individuals affected by the actions of the powerful, emphasizing the importance of social responsibility.

Language Analysis: The repetition of "millions" underscores the vast number of people impacted by the actions of those in power, highlighting the need for empathy and accountability.

Historical Context: This quote speaks to the growing awareness of the consequences of power and authority in early 20th century England, as society grappled with the effects of social inequality and moral corruption.

6. *"You have no power to make me change my mind."*

Meaning: Mrs. Birling asserts her independence and authority, refusing to be swayed by the Inspector's arguments.

Language Analysis: The phrase "no power" highlights Mrs. Birling's defiance and determination to maintain control over her own decisions and beliefs.

Historical Context: This quote illustrates the resistance to change and accountability among the older generation in early 20th century England, as they cling to their traditional values and sense of power.

7. *"He's giving us the rope – so that we'll hang ourselves."*

Meaning: Sheila recognizes the Inspector's strategy of allowing the Birlings to reveal their own guilt, highlighting his power and authority over the situation.

Language Analysis: The metaphor of "giving us the rope" and "hang ourselves" emphasizes the Inspector's control and manipulation of the situation, illustrating his ability to expose the Birlings' guilt and moral failings.

Historical Context: This quote reflects the shifting power dynamics in early 20th century England, as individuals in positions of authority were increasingly held accountable for their actions and the consequences they had on others.

8. *"I was in a furious temper. I went to the manager at Milwards and I told him that if they didn't get rid of that girl, I'd never go near the place again and I'd persuade mother to close our account with them."*

Meaning: Sheila uses her social status and influence to exert power over Eva Smith's employment, demonstrating the devastating impact of authority when misused.

Language Analysis: The phrases "furious temper" and "get rid of that girl" illustrate the impulsive and destructive nature of Sheila's actions, highlighting the potential consequences of unchecked power.

Historical Context: This quote exposes the power dynamics between the upper and working classes in early 20th century England, revealing the ease with which the wealthy could exploit and manipulate those beneath them.

9. *"It's a free country, I told them."*

Meaning: Eric defends his right to express his opinion, asserting his belief in individual freedom and autonomy.

Language Analysis: The phrase "free country" underscores Eric's belief in the importance of personal freedom and the right to challenge authority. The short sentence helps emphasis this point.

Historical Context: This quote reflects the growing demand for individual autonomy and freedom of expression in early 20th century England, as younger generations began to challenge traditional power structures and values.

10. "I don't come into this suicide business."

Meaning: Mrs. Birling attempts to distance herself from Eva Smith's death, refusing to accept any responsibility or acknowledge her power to impact others.

Language Analysis: The phrase "suicide business" minimizes the gravity of Eva Smith's death, emphasizing Mrs. Birling's denial and lack of empathy.

Historical Context: This quote highlights the resistance to acknowledging the consequences of power and authority among the older generation in early 20th century England, as they struggled to come to terms with the changing values and expectations surrounding social responsibility.

5) LANGUAGE TECHNIQUES

In "An Inspector Calls", Priestley uses a number of different language techniques to help emphasize his points and engage the audience. It's important you understand these different techniques, and the impact they have on the play.

For all exam boards, you are required to provide language analysis (AO2) to support your quotes. This is quite a large chunk of your entire marks for the essay. We've already given you various different bits of language analysis in previous chapters, but what about the specific language techniques?

In this section, we list 25 of the major language techniques you need to know, and give an example of each from "An Inspector Calls".

Alliteration: Repetition of consonant sounds at the beginning of words for emphasis or creating a specific effect.

Example: "Burnt her inside out, of course" – The repetition of the "b" sound emphasizes the brutality of Eva's death.

Hyperbole: Exaggeration used to create emphasis or effect.

Example: "Millions and millions of Eva Smiths and John Smiths" – The Inspector uses hyperbole to stress the vast number of people affected by the Birlings' actions.

Simile: A comparison between two things using "like" or "as."

Example: "She was here alone, like a helpless animal" – The comparison of Eva to a helpless animal evokes sympathy and highlights her vulnerability.

Metaphor: A direct comparison between two things without using "like" or "as."

Example: "We are members of one body" – The metaphor represents society as a single, interconnected organism.

Personification: Assigning human qualities to non-human entities or objects.

Example: "The Titanic – she sails next week" – Describing the Titanic as "she" personifies the ship, making it seem more relatable and significant.

Irony: A contrast between what is said and what is meant or what is expected and what occurs.

Example: "Unsinkable, absolutely unsinkable" – Mr. Birling's ironic statement about the Titanic foreshadows the ship's eventual sinking.

Foreshadowing: Hints or clues about future events in the story.

Example: The Inspector's arrival interrupts Mr. Birling's speech about personal responsibility, foreshadowing the events that follow.

Repetition: Repeating words or phrases for emphasis or effect.

Example: "You're not the kind of father a chap could go to when he's in trouble" – Eric's repetition of "father" emphasizes his disappointment in Mr. Birling.

Imagery: Descriptive language that appeals to the senses.

Example: "Two hours ago a young woman died in the infirmary. She'd been taken there because she'd swallowed a lot of strong disinfectant." – The vivid description helps the reader visualize the gruesome scene.

Symbolism: Using objects or actions to represent abstract ideas or concepts.

Example: The Inspector's name, "Goole," symbolizes his ghostly, mysterious nature and his role as a moral judge.

Pathetic fallacy: Attributing human emotions or characteristics to nature or inanimate objects to reflect characters' emotions.

Example: The play's setting in the Birling's dining room represents their isolation and detachment from the outside world.

Juxtaposition: Placing contrasting ideas or elements next to each other to create emphasis or effect.

Example: The contrast between the Birlings' celebratory atmosphere and the Inspector's arrival underscores the difference between their private lives and public responsibilities.

Oxymoron: Combining two contradictory terms to create a new meaning.

Example: "You're beginning to pretend now that nothing's really happened at all" – Sheila accuses her family of "pretending" to be innocent, suggesting their guilt.

Onomatopoeia: Words that imitate the sounds they represent.

Example: "The sharp ring of a front doorbell" – The onomatopoeia "ring" emphasizes the sudden and unexpected arrival of the Inspector.

Parallelism: Using similar grammatical structures or sentence patterns for emphasis or effect.

Example: "We don't live alone. We are members of one body. We are responsible for each other." – The parallel structure highlights the message of interconnectedness.

Anaphora: Repetition of a word or phrase at the beginning of successive sentences or clauses for emphasis.

Example: "But just remember this. One Eva Smith has gone – but there are millions and millions and millions of Eva Smiths and John Smiths" – The repetition of "millions" emphasizes the vast number of people affected by the Birlings' actions.

Epiphora: Repetition of a word or phrase at the end of successive sentences or clauses for emphasis.

Example: "We are responsible for each other. And I tell you that the time will soon come when, if men will not learn that lesson, then they will be taught it in fire and blood and anguish." – The repetition of "and" builds tension and reinforces the Inspector's message of social responsibility.

Rhetorical question: A question posed for effect rather than requiring an answer.

Example: "And you think young women ought to be protected against unpleasant and disturbing things?" – The Inspector's rhetorical question challenges Mrs. Birling's hypocrisy and forces her to consider the consequences of her actions.

Assonance: Repetition of vowel sounds within words for emphasis or creating a specific effect.

Example: "Look, Inspector – I'd give thousands – yes, thousands" – The repetition of the "ou" sound reinforces Mr. Birling's desperation to absolve himself of guilt.

Litotes: An understatement created by denying the opposite of the intended meaning.

Example: "You're not quite so important now, are you?" – Sheila's litotes highlights Mr. Birling's diminished authority in the face of the Inspector's revelations.

Sarcasm: A cutting, often ironic remark intended to wound or mock.

Example: "I suppose we're all nice people now" – Sheila's sarcastic comment underscores the moral hypocrisy of her family.

Caesura: A pause or break in a line of poetry, often used for dramatic effect.

Example: "But take my word for it, you youngsters – and I've learnt in the good hard school of experience – that a man has to mind his own business and look after himself and his own" – The caesura in Mr. Birling's speech emphasizes his belief in self-reliance.

Paradox: A statement that seems contradictory but reveals a deeper truth.

Example: "It's the only time I've ever done anything like that, and I'll never, never do it again to anybody" – Sheila's paradoxical statement highlights her remorse and newfound understanding of her responsibility to others.

Pun: A play on words that exploits the multiple meanings or similar sounds of words for humorous or rhetorical effect.

Example: "It's better to ask for the earth than to take it" – The Inspector's pun on "ask for the earth" (meaning to make excessive demands) and "take it" (meaning to exploit resources) emphasizes the importance of social responsibility.

Synecdoche: Using a part of something to represent the whole or vice versa.

Example: "You lot may be letting yourselves out nicely, but I can't" – The use of "lot" to represent the entire Birling family emphasizes their collective guilt and responsibility.

6) EXAMPLE ESSAY QUESTIONS

Here are some example questions that you could be asked at GCSE level. These are based on previous questions for exam boards AQA and Edexcel, but they are NOT past questions, they simply follow a similar structure.

1. *Explore how Priestley presents the theme of social class in "An Inspector Calls."*

2. *Discuss the significance of the Inspector's final speech in the play.*

3. *How does Priestley use the character of Mr. Birling to criticize capitalist values?*

4. *Analyze the role of women in "An Inspector Calls" and discuss how Priestley critiques gender roles.*

5. *How does Priestley create tension and suspense through the structure of "An Inspector Calls"?*

6. Discuss the theme of guilt and responsibility in "An Inspector Calls."

7. How does the character of Gerald Croft reflect the values of the time period in "An Inspector Calls"?

8. Explore the role of deception and secrecy in "An Inspector Calls."

9. How does Priestley use the character of Eva Smith to explore the consequences of social inequality?

10. Discuss the importance of morality and ethics in "An Inspector Calls."

11. How does Priestley convey the theme of power and authority in "An Inspector Calls"?

12. Analyze the relationship between Eric and his parents in "An Inspector Calls."

13. How does Priestley use foreshadowing in "An Inspector Calls"?

14. Examine the portrayal of family dynamics in "An Inspector Calls."

15. Discuss the theme of ignorance and its consequences in "An Inspector Calls."

16. How does Priestley use symbolism in "An

Inspector Calls" to convey his message?

17. Explore the character of Mrs. Birling and her role in the play.

18. How does Priestley portray the consequences of selfishness in "An Inspector Calls"?

19. Analyze the theme of change and transformation in "An Inspector Calls."

20. Discuss the role of justice and judgment in "An Inspector Calls."

21. How does Priestley use language techniques to emphasize themes in "An Inspector Calls"?

22. Explore the impact of the Inspector's arrival on the Birling family in "An Inspector Calls."

23. Analyze the significance of the setting in "An Inspector Calls."

24. How does Priestley use the theme of truth and lies to convey his message in "An Inspector Calls"?

25. Discuss the importance of timing in the events of "An Inspector Calls."

Remember that when answering these questions, you should provide a clear argument, analyze specific evidence from the text (including quotations), and structure your response coherently, ensuring your arguments are well-supported and logically presented.

Have a go at answering some of these questions. If the question is about a theme you haven't studied, try to link it to a theme (or a character) that you know well. There are always ways to link your answers. You will also always have a choice of questions, so if a horrible one comes up, you won't have to answer it!

7) MARK SCHEME

For GCSE English, most exam boards have a similar mark scheme. Here is a basic summary.

AO1 – Answer the question, use quotes throughout

AO2 – Analyse the language and structure using relevant terminology

AO3 – Use context

AO4 – Vocabulary, spelling punctuation

First of all, they want you to answer the question in a clear and concise way. Make sure you refer back to the question in each paragraph, and use quotes to back up your arguments, in order to get full marks in this section.

Secondly, don't just give quotes. You need to analyse them (using the terminology discussed earlier in this book). How do the language techniques / wording choices help to further the discussion? How would they impact the audience?

Thirdly, use historical context (again, this was discussed in previous chapters). How does each quote/character/theme relate to the historical context of the time?

Lastly, be sure to use a range of vocabulary, sentence structure, and spell correctly. This is worth less marks, but still important!

The easiest way to get full marks at GCSE is to have a good structure to your essay.

Firstly, write an introduction that answers the question, gives your argument, and briefly explains what you are going to talk about in your essay. If you can include a bit of historical context in the intro, even better.

Secondly you want to do 3-5 paragraphs, each one based around a different character, theme, or idea. In each of these paragraphs, you need to answer the question, give quotes, analyse the quotes, and mention some context. Basically include AO1, AO2, AO3 in each paragraph.

Finally, write a small conclusion that reinforces your answer and concludes your essay. Easy!

In general, questions either ask you about a character

or a theme (mostly). A great tip is this: If you answer a character question, do each paragraph on a different theme (that relates to the character). If you answer a theme question, do each paragraph on a different character (that relates to the theme). This isn't always the case, but is a good rule of thumb that can help you structure your answers.

8) EXAMPLE ANSWERS

Here are a couple of Grade 9 / top mark example answers for "An Inspector Calls". **You won't have to write this well** in order to achieve top grades, but it's just to give you an example of the type of thing you should be including.

These answers are **far longer** than you will have to write in an exam, but it's useful to make them longer here in order for you to get more ideas to use in your own work. You also won't need to give the exact Acts or lines that the quotes were from, we've just done that to help you find the quotes if you like.

For each of these answers, remember to look out for AO1 (answering the question), AO2 (analysing quotes), and AO3 (historical context).

Explore how Priestley presents the theme of social class in "An Inspector Calls."

In "An Inspector Calls," J.B. Priestley presents the theme of social class through the attitudes and actions of the characters, their interactions, and the consequences of their behavior. The play, set in 1912, critiques the rigid class system in place in Edwardian England and highlights the negative consequences of its values. Through the characters' dialogue, actions, and the Inspector's revelations, Priestley exposes the injustices and hypocrisy of the upper class and emphasizes the need for social responsibility and change.

Priestley uses Mr. Birling, the patriarch of the Birling family, as a representation of the upper class's self-interest and disregard for the lower classes. This is evident in Mr. Birling's speeches, where he often champions capitalist values, such as when he states that "a man has to mind his own business and look after himself and his own." This quote demonstrates the selfish attitude of the upper class, who prioritize their own interests over the well-being of others. The use of imperatives such as "mind" and "look after" emphasizes Mr. Birling's insistence on self-preservation, while the repetition of "his own" highlights his narrow-mindedness. Additionally, Mr. Birling's language and tone throughout the play are condescending towards those of lower social standing, such as when he refers to Eva Smith as a "girl of that class." The use of the determiner "that" highlights the dismissive attitude of the upper class towards the working class, positioning them as inferior and unworthy of consideration.

The character of Mrs. Birling further reinforces the theme of social class through her arrogance and self-righteousness. As the wife of a wealthy businessman and a member of influential women's organizations, Mrs. Birling occupies a high social position, which she uses to justify her cruel treatment of Eva Smith. When discussing her refusal to help Eva, Mrs. Birling claims that "she had only herself to blame." The pronoun "she" distances Mrs. Birling from the girl, while the phrase "only herself to blame" suggests that the responsibility for her misfortunes lies solely with Eva, absolving the upper class of any wrongdoing. This attitude exemplifies the Edwardian class system's rigidity, which allowed the privileged few to wield power over the vulnerable many without consequence.

In contrast, the characters of Sheila and Eric Birling represent a more compassionate and self-aware perspective on social class. Their initial ignorance of the implications of their actions highlights the moral blindness of the upper class; however, as the play progresses, they begin to understand the consequences of their actions and accept responsibility for them. For example, Sheila's remorseful statement, "I'll never, never do it again to anybody," demonstrates her newfound awareness of her actions' impact on others, regardless of their social class. The repetition of "never" emphasizes her commitment to change and highlights the potential for the younger generation to break free from the class system's constraints.

The character of Inspector Goole serves as the catalyst for the play's exploration of social class. His questioning of the characters and the subsequent revelations about their mistreatment of Eva Smith force them to confront the consequences of their actions, exposing the class system's inherent injustices. The Inspector's impassioned speech, in which he argues that "we are members of one body," advocates for a sense of social responsibility and collective guilt that transcends class boundaries. The metaphor of "one body" emphasizes the interconnectedness of all members of society, regardless of their social status, and highlights the need for empathy and compassion.

In conclusion, J.B. Priestley presents the theme of social class in "An Inspector Calls" through the attitudes, actions, and interactions of the characters, as well as the Inspector's revelations. By exploring the injustices and hypocrisy of the upper class and advocating for social responsibility and change, Priestley critiques the rigid class system of Edwardian England. Through the characters' language and actions, he exposes the consequences of their behavior on those of lower social standing, highlighting the need for compassion and empathy to transcend social divisions.

Explore the character of Mrs. Birling and her role in the play.

In "An Inspector Calls," J.B. Priestley uses the character of Mrs. Birling to explore the attitudes and values of the upper class in Edwardian England. As the wife of a successful businessman and a member of influential women's organizations, Mrs. Birling represents the traditional, conservative values of her time. Through her actions, dialogue, and interactions with other characters, Priestley highlights the hypocrisy and moral failings of the upper class and emphasizes the need for change.

Mrs. Birling's character is defined by her self-righteousness and arrogance, which are evident in her interactions with other characters. Her condescending manner is most apparent in her conversations with the Inspector, as she tries to assert her social superiority over him. For instance, when the Inspector questions her about her involvement in Eva Smith's case, she asserts, "You have no power to make me change my mind." This statement emphasizes her belief in her own infallibility and showcases her unwillingness to accept responsibility for her actions. The use of the words "no power" highlights her belief in her own authority, a result of her privileged social status.

Furthermore, Mrs. Birling's lack of empathy towards those of lower social standing is illustrated through her refusal to help Eva Smith. When describing her encounter with Eva, she states, "I did nothing I'm ashamed of." This quote demonstrates Mrs. Birling's inability to recognize the consequences of her actions, as well as her unwillingness to accept any blame for the young woman's tragic fate. The use of the word "ashamed" highlights her belief that she acted morally and within her rights, further illustrating her self-righteous nature.

The character of Mrs. Birling also serves to expose the hypocrisy of the upper class. Despite her apparent devotion to charitable work, Mrs. Birling's actions reveal her true motivations: maintaining her social status and upholding the values of her class. This is exemplified by her treatment of Eva Smith, whom she dismisses as "impertinent" and "not deserving of any assistance." This portrayal of Mrs. Birling as a hypocrite underscores the play's central theme of social responsibility and the consequences of failing to acknowledge it.

In addition to her function as a representation of the upper class's moral failings, Mrs. Birling's character also contributes to the play's exploration of gender roles. As a woman in Edwardian society, her role is confined to that of a wife, mother, and socialite. This is demonstrated by her concern with maintaining appearances and her adherence to traditional gender roles. For example, when her daughter Sheila expresses her opinions and emotions openly, Mrs. Birling chastises her, saying, "You'll have to get used to that, just as I had." This quote suggests that women of Mrs. Birling's generation were expected to suppress their feelings and accept their subservient roles in society.

However, Mrs. Birling's character also serves as a foil to the younger, more progressive characters in the play, such as Sheila and Eric. Their growth and development throughout the play highlight the potential for change within society, in contrast to the rigid and unchanging values exemplified by Mrs. Birling.

In conclusion, the character of Mrs. Birling in "An Inspector Calls" serves to explore the attitudes and values of the upper class in Edwardian England. Through her actions, dialogue, and interactions with other characters, Priestley highlights the hypocrisy and moral failings of the upper class, as well as the societal expectations placed on women in early 20th Century England. By contrasting her character with the more empathetic and progressive younger characters, Priestley emphasizes the need for change and the potential for a more just and equitable society.

9) GOOD LUCK

That's it! English essays, particularly at GCSE level, are all about providing clear, concise arguments that follow the mark scheme. You don't have to say anything complex to get high marks, as long as you answer the question and tackle the infamous AOs.

Overall, "An Inspector Calls" covers a variety of important themes surrounding important topics such as class and power, which makes it easier than most to hit the context (AO3) marks. It doesn't have quite as much language points as in a Shakespeare play, but it has enough powerful imagery to be able to talk about in detail for your AO2 marks.

Once you learn the major quotes, including some contextual and language analysis, then your most of the way there. After that, it's all about practice, practice, practice. Do some practice papers, mark them yourself, and just keep going until you get there. Good luck!

Printed in Great Britain
by Amazon